CELEBRATING THE FAMILY NAME OF HARRIS

Celebrating the Family Name of Harris

Walter the Educator

Silent King Books
a WhichHead Entertainment Imprint

Copyright © 2024 by Walter the Educator

All rights reserved. No part of this book may be reproduced in any manner whatsoever without written permission except in the case of brief quotations embodied in critical articles and reviews.

First Printing, 2024

Disclaimer

This book is a literary work; the story is not about specific persons, locations, situations, and/or circumstances unless mentioned in a historical context. Any resemblance to real persons, locations, situations, and/or circumstances is coincidental. This book is for entertainment and informational purposes only. The author and publisher offer this information without warranties expressed or implied. No matter the grounds, neither the author nor the publisher will be accountable for any losses, injuries, or other damages caused by the reader's use of this book. The use of this book acknowledges an understanding and acceptance of this disclaimer.

Celebrating the Family Name of Harris is a memory book that belongs to the Celebrating Family Name Book Series by Walter the Educator. Collect them all and more books at WaltertheEducator.com

USE THE EXTRA SPACE TO DOCUMENT YOUR FAMILY MEMORIES THROUGHOUT THE YEARS

HARRIS

In rolling hills where wildflowers bloom,
Celebrating the Family Name of

Harris

And twilight casts a gentle gloom,

The name of Harris rises proud,

A whisper soft, yet clear and loud.

From roots that dig in fertile earth,

To branches wide, the Harris birth,

Of family strong and hearts so true,

In every breath, a spirit new.

They came with dreams as vast as skies,

With courage bold, and knowing eyes,

Through every storm, through every test,

The name of Harris stood the best.

In fields of gold and oceans wide,

Wherever Harris did abide,

They left a mark, a trail of light,

A legacy that shines so bright.

Celebrating the Family Name of

Harris

With hands that built and hearts that healed,

In every task, the Harris sealed,

A bond of love, a trust so deep,

In every vow, in every leap.

The children of the Harris name,

In every game, in every aim,

They carry forth the torch of old,

With stories rich and tales untold.

Through winters cold and summers long,

The Harris heart beats ever strong,

With laughter ringing through the years,

And eyes that chase away all fears.

In every dawn, in every night,

The name of Harris holds the light,

A beacon on the roughest seas,

Celebrating the Family Name of

Harris

A name that brings the world to ease.

Through trials faced and battles won,

The Harris legacy goes on,

With every step, a trail they blaze,

A testament to brighter days.

The winds may shift, the times may change,

But Harris holds, with range and range,

A family bound by ties that last,

Celebrating the Family Name of

Harris

A present rich with echoes past.

ABOUT THE CREATOR

Walter the Educator is one of the pseudonyms for Walter Anderson. Formally educated in Chemistry, Business, and Education, he is an educator, an author, a diverse entrepreneur, and he is the son of a disabled war veteran. "Walter the Educator" shares his time between educating and creating. He holds interests and owns several creative projects that entertain, enlighten, enhance, and educate, hoping to inspire and motivate you. Follow, find new works, and stay up to date with Walter the Educator™

at WaltertheEducator.com

www.ingramcontent.com/pod-product-compliance
Lightning Source LLC
LaVergne TN
LVHW012051070526
838201LV00082B/3910